THE MOUNTAIN

Laura Ding-Edwards

ISBN - 978-1-912779-90-1 (Print)
ISBN - 978-1-912779-91-8 (Ebook)

Book Design by Michael Maloney

Cover illustration by Laura Ding-Edwards

First edition published in 2019

That Guy's House
20-22 Wenlock Road
London
England
N1 7GU

www.ThatGuysHouse.com

For my parents, husband and best friends – thank you for sitting with me in the dark and dancing with me in the light.

Praise for

Laura Ding-Edwards' work;

"Woven within her evocative words are teachings that give life to the places within us only few dare to breathe"

"Like having a friend coming to sit quietly beside you and whispering everything will be ok"

"Poems that bring peace and healing to a troubled mind"

"Reading her work is like a warm, tight hug seen by your eyes but felt in the deepest parts of your soul"

"A special talent for capturing the thoughts and feelings of all who are struggling and putting them into words that are uniquely beautiful and comforting"

"Laura's work has helped me immensely, I believe her audience loves the authenticity and connection with her"

"The wisdom that our hearts are trying to tell our minds"

"I truly, truly believe these poems have saved a loved ones life – the power of Laura's words gave them hope, recognition and a pathway into how they were able to express their feelings"

"Some of the most important writing I've ever had the honour of reading"

Contents

Poems

Prose

Foreword

Thank you for being here with my book, I am so grateful. Whether it's been gifted, borrowed or you've spent your hard earned money on it, thank you for spending your precious time on the words I've written, every single one of you has a piece of my heart.

This is not a self help book. It's not a cure for anything. It's not a profound story of how I've beaten mental illness or found enlightenment. It is a raw, honest, real documentation of being human. I have been entirely lucky that the words have resonated with people and given comfort and hope. For me, that is the ultimate in giving back. I don't have the answers but I will lay my heart bare for you to see and take what you need to feel like you're not alone in your battles, whatever they look like.

The poems and prose I've written weave through many subjects; anxiety, friendship, heartbreak, depression, body image, the media, love and hate.

The overarching message, I hope, is that perfection is unattainable, kindness is imperative and embracing every part of who we are is the only way we find any kind of peace within ourselves. Working to change the bits of us that aren't helpful, nurturing the parts of us that are good and being brave enough to say "this is me; I am enough".

I really hope you enjoy what you're about to read and that you are able to take something from the parts of me I've shared with you.

With love,
Laura xx

Poems

Laura Ding-Edwards

x

The Mountain

If the mountain seems too big today
Then climb a hill instead
If the morning brings you sadness
It's ok to stay in bed
If the day ahead weighs heavy
And your plans feel like a curse
There's no shame in rearranging
Don't make yourself feel worse
If a shower stings like needles
And a bath feels like you'll drown
If you haven't washed your hair for days
Don't throw away your crown
A day is not a lifetime
A rest is not defeat
Don't think of it as failure
Just a quiet kind retreat
The mountain will still be there
When you want to try again
You can climb it in your own time
Just love yourself 'til then.

Laura Ding-Edwards

Angel

Your words weigh much more than your body
Your heart will reflect on your face
Your soul bears the scars
Of the world's fallen stars
And the cruelty of the human race

Your hands have healed more than you realise
Your smile has warmed hearts you've not met
Your listening ears;
Shoulders dampened with tears
Are the gift you give without debt

Your arms have embraced broken spirits
Those shattered, and giving up hope
Your kindness has eased
The buckling knees
Of people that cried *"I can't cope"*

The size of your house and your fortune
Has nothing to do with your worth
Your things and possessions
Aren't stories or lessons
You can only count money on Earth

Look after the gifts you've been given
You beautiful, kind-hearted thing
Love all, not a few
But mostly, love you
An angel can't fly with one wing

We Are

We are battered, but not broken
We are weary, worn and scarred
We are tearful, we are tired
We are constantly on guard
We are wounded, we are bleeding
We are stranded, lost at sea
We are caged, and we are crippled
We are desperate to be free
We are full and yet so empty
We are tired but can't sleep
We are functioning on nothing
We are drowning in the deep
We are winning though; have heart
We are surviving as a pack
We are not here to surrender
We are always fighting back
We are bruised but not defeated
We are down, but not yet out
We are one almighty force
We are worthy, there's no doubt
We are strong and we are fierce
We are capable, we've shown
We are part of something bigger
We are not in this alone

One

A love of power reigns supreme
And unity is just a dream
And pitchforks pile hate on hate
And no-one can negotiate

A decent wage for everyone
And foodbanks that aren't overrun
With nurses on their seventh freeze
An NHS that's on its knees

Where such loss of humanity
Sparks a viral effigy
Of people trapped in burning towers
Where families lay forlorn flowers

And children drowned in UK seas
Are seen as no more than disease
And families escaping plight
Are met with cries of *"shoot on sight"*

Media owned by billionaires
Who shove their cash in stocks and shares
Of companies that benefit
From the fallout of a hard Brexit

And so they tell us who to hate
To keep us in our morbid state
Of blaming those less fortunate
The curse of the subordinate

Divide and conquer is the aim
So let's destroy their wicked game
And start a movement in its place
Uprising of the human race

Where hope is King, compassion Queen
The unity we dared to dream
New dawn begins, we are the prequel
One race
One love
One world
One people

Laura Ding-Edwards

The Honest Truth

Be kind, but know the honest truth
Protect yourself as well
Not everyone you find in life
Will meet you parallel
Not all who come to you for love
Will give love in return
Not every fire lit will warm
Some only serve to burn
Not every broken heart you hold
Is ready to start feeling
Not everyone who carries pain
Is able to start healing
Not everyone who walks with you
Will wait if you're too slow
Not everyone will catch you up
Some have too far to go
Not all who you place in your heart
Will treat it with respect
Some will trample and destroy it
Due to their own defect
Be kind wherever possible
But please do not forget
Not everyone is ready
To receive your kindness yet

You

Look after the You you've been given

You're the only You you'll get

The best around

The best I've found

There isn't another You yet

Laura Ding-Edwards

Beautifully Strange

Don't judge me on my failures;
All the times that I've said no
I'm much more than
A cancelled plan
Just give me room to grow

Don't judge me from a distance
"She doesn't look depressed"
I did my hair
While I still care
Some days I don't get dressed

Don't judge me for my bad days
I'm not ignoring you
Sometimes the tone
Of a ringing phone
Sends adrenaline coursing through

Don't judge me by my photos
I'm not a selfie queen
Don't berate
Please celebrate
When I want to be seen

Don't judge me on my weight or size
It doesn't equal worth
Fat or thin
Beauty's within
We all belong on earth

Don't judge unless you've been there

It's not that hard to change

The harsh critique

To *"we're unique"*

And beautifully strange

Laura Ding-Edwards

Thirty-Five

I am thirty-five years of survival

My size four feet have walked alone

And behind

And beside

My rough hands have held

Soothed

Hit and hardened

Healed

My ears have listened and learned

Heard and ignored

My mouth has kissed

Poisoned

Apologised and pleaded

Pretended

Defended

Spoken softly and sharply

My eyes have wrinkled with laughter

Happy drought lines

Ingrained where young tears flooded, fell

And finally faded

My heart keeps secrets and stories

Lovers

And enemies

Broken and beaten and stolen

And repaired

I am every minute of my being

Every chapter of my story

Every beginning

Middle and

End

Warrior

When the world is on your shoulders
And your heart feels full of lead
And your stomach churns like butter
And the voice inside your head
Is reminding you of everything
You've ever said or done
All your failures and regrets
And all the times your fear has won
Take a minute to remember
You've survived all this before
You've battled and you've conquered
When you thought you had no more
You are stronger than you realise
You are brave and wise and kind
And you know you're so much bigger
Than the doubts that fill your mind
So breathe it in then let it out
Allow the ebb and flow
You can win this war, you always do
You're a warrior you know

Laura Ding-Edwards

Hate Me

You can hate me from a distance
You can mock me to my face
You can throw me all your anger
But you're choosing the wrong place

You can sting me with your venom
You can drag my name through dirt
You can make up lies and stories
It's not me they're going to hurt

You can twist and you can tamper
You can form your own story
You can cast and you can reel
You won't get a bite from me

You can shame and you can shade me
You can break and bend and bleed
You can blame it on me all you like
I hope one day you're freed

From the bitterness of hatred
And your dark hostility
The red-hot coals you carry round
Are not blistering me

So pile it all on me, my friend
One day your pain may cease
'Til then you choose your chaos
And I will choose my peace

Fight

Depression isn't blindness
We are still able to see
But cannot find the match to spark
Our own ability

Depression isn't darkness
Soft, familiar and full
But a groggy, heavy seascape
With a fatal tidal pull

Depression isn't empty
For emptiness is space
A luxury no longer known
A bleak yet florid place

Depression isn't sadness
Tears bring no relief
And no amount of mourning
Can process unnamed grief

Depression is not sorry
Nor remorseful of its curse
It is ruthless, rough, repetitive
Fixed on making you feel worse

Depression is not weakness
It will floor the strongest man
A silent, sly assassin
Fight – I know you can

Laura Ding-Edwards

The 84

One's your local postman
Sat in his van in tears
One is an old school friend
Who you haven't seen for years
One is driving taxis
Hearing tales of joy and woe
One feels like he's nothing
Because so many told him so
One is hitting adulthood
With so much more ahead
He should be planning life
But he is planning death instead
One is sleeping rough: -
Days and nights of ignorance
Things could have been so different
If he'd been noticed, even once
One is so successful
Yet the world is often blind
Money, homes and holidays
Can't cure a broken mind
One's always invited;
The life and soul - last one to bed
The sex and drugs and drink
Drown out the screaming in his head
One is writing letters
Tying up all the loose ends
Ironic, really
Seeing as he felt he had no friends
One is back from service
He is trying to adjust

To normality and family

Not guns and blood and dust

One is breaking

One is broken

One is sorry

One is lost

One is reading

One is thinking

One will fight at any cost

One is sitting, waiting

For the tiny glow of hope

And one is reaching out to you, admitting he can't cope

We can't forget the men, when we're discussing mental health

The clue is in the title – boys, please don't lose yourself

In the toxic social stigma of manning up and keeping on

There's no shame in speaking up and not pretending to be strong

So heads up, we are here to lift your heart up off the floor

Reach out and take our hands

Don't become one of eighty-four

Laura Ding-Edwards

Remedy

"Sticks and stones may break my bones
But names will never hurt me"
But we all bear the scars of words
So brutal, heartless – dirty

The physical feels easy
Just a simple fix and rest
But words are barbed and poisonous
Blades plunged into your chest

They penetrate your spirit
Bore a hole into your heart
Infect your confidence and
Halt your dreams before they start

A parasite, bacteria
A savage, stubborn stain
A venomous arachnid
Spinning webs within your brain

You hold your pain and anger
And your bitterness inside
It only serves to burn you
Broken heart, acidifed

You have amazing power, though
To stop the septic spread
Of the false, malicious narrative
That echoes round your head

The lies that you've been told
Of your integrity and value
Are just old tales of monsters
Who are waiting to devour you

Treat your heart with love
Shine a light into your soul
Change your inner dialogue
And take back your control

You're older now and wiser
You're strong and wild and tough
So find the peace within you
And believe you are enough

Forgiving those who hurt you
Is the only remedy
Pour water onto poison
And dilute toxicity

Laura Ding-Edwards

Circus

My mind is like a circus; filled with bicycles and clowns
A cacophony of noise; guests from visitors and towns

A dancer shines in sequins, on a prancing bright white horse
A juggler, an acrobat, no room here for remorse

And here I stand; the Ringmaster, directing my display
But sometimes in the midst of it, it swings the other way

The lions breach their cages; the elephants escape
The lighting shifts from bright to black – the circus changes shape

A desolate arena, no visitors or friends
Just a lonely lost director; no starts, middles or ends

Surrounded by the darkness big cats growl and pace and claw
No smiling happy faces; no spectacular encore

I take myself to safety - wait it out, it won't be long
Until the lions have retreated, and I'm back where I belong

It only takes one person; a friendly welcome face
To extend a hand and help me up - with dignity and grace

The colours start returning, and the mood begins to lift
The seats fill up with friends again; their company a gift

I stand again as master of the circus in my mind
Start my show with the reminder – *"it's important to be kind"*

Love Is

Love

Real love

Real love is a movement

It's equal, yet not fixed

It moves and rebalances

Nothing owed

Nothing gained

Just a slow

Steady

Sway of weight

From one

To the other

And back

Laura Ding-Edwards

This Is Me

You're not how much you weigh
Or what you choose to wear
You're not your inner thigh gap
Or the way you do your hair
You're not your flabby tummy
Or the bags under your eyes
Your eyebrows are just perfect
And your boobs aren't the wrong size
You're not your disability
Or fragile mental state
You don't choose to have an illness
And it's not up for debate
You're not your sexuality
Your gender or your race
Your worth has no relation
To who you fall for, or your face
You're all the little pieces
Of the things you see and do
What you learn from what you suffer
Is how you become you
Place weight onto your kindness
Choose love and loyalty
See your realness in the mirror
And with pride say *"this is me"*

The Horse

It was twilight in December; not a leaf upon a tree,
A little girl lay sleeping, she was not much more than three,
Stirring from her slumber, silver moon upon her face,
She tiptoed to the window; drew the curtain made of lace

At the bottom of the garden, where the boundary met the wood,
A horse was quietly standing; he looked kind and calm and good,
He stopped what he was doing and looked up towards the girl,
"There's magic in the air," she thought and tucked a stray blonde curl,

She watched him turn towards the wood, and heard him softly say,
"Don't worry Girl, I'm going, but I'll return another day."
She closed the curtain quickly, and jumped back into her bed,
Pulled the covers up on top of her - lay down her little head.

She was five the next she saw him, standing in his usual place,
He nickered to her softly, and she understood his face,
She climbed down from the window; dewy grass on her bare feet,
And walked eagerly towards the horse, so they could truly meet,

"Oh Horse," she exclaimed, smiling *"I'm so happy you returned!"*
"I started school this year; you won't believe the things I've learned!"
The horse nudged at her shoulder, and then whispered in her ear,
"The world is full of wonder; there's much to learn while we are here"

Another seven years had passed before he next stopped by,
She told him tales of high school, and the girls who'd made her cry,
The horse had dropped his head to hers and told her quietly,
"My Girl, it's hard, but you will find that kindness is the key"

The next time he appeared was on the cusp of womanhood,
Aged barely seventeen, young grace and beauty where she stood,
She cried and told him of the boy who broke her fragile heart,
He replied by simply saying *"Love is a complicated art."*

The girl was not a girl at all when he had next stopped by,
But something seemed to trouble him; she couldn't work out why?
"What is the matter Horse, you seem so distant and depressed –
Are you tired or unwell? Come, lie down here and have a rest."

He looked at her with sorrow, took a moment to reply,
"Girl, I am so sorry, but it's time to say goodbye –
My bones are old and frail, and my muscles are so sore,
I wish that it was different, but I can't visit anymore."

Her eyes prickled with silent tears; her chest began to hurt,
Her knees gave way beneath her, and she crumpled to the dirt,
"You can't leave Horse, I need you, you're my best friend," she cried
And then he heard sobs tumble from the little girl inside

"I know that you will miss me, Girl, it's just what I must do
One day, so many years from now, you'll feel this aching too.
I promise I won't be too far, just beyond the wood,
In a place of endless peace where all is kind and calm and good"

She pressed her face into his neck, until her tears ran dry,
She kissed his forelock gently, as she choked out *"Horse, goodbye"*
Then she watched him walk away, into the darkness of the trees,
As swallows surfed in circles, on the evening summer breeze

Sometimes in the twilight when the world was dark and still
She'd hear the sound of whinnying beyond the farthest hill

And often in the woodland while she ambled through the green
She was sure she could hear galloping, yet nothing could be seen

A little while had passed when, in a dream, a well-known face
"I've come to let you know" Horse said *"I've reached my resting place"*
"All is well with me, I'm young and wild again – I'm free.
I'll wait here Girl until the day you come and follow me"

The Things I Can't Do

The things I can't do make up the best parts of me

I can't go in a lift
But I can raise spirits that are downtrodden, empty and solemn

I can't travel far
But I can show you places in your soul you didn't believe existed

I can't fly
But I can fix your wings and watch you soar

I can't stop feeling
But I will feel everything with you, so you're not alone

I can't sleep
So I will sit with you under the blanket of your twisted, tormented
nights
And wait for the light to come

I can't forget
But I will create memories with you that mean we never want to

I can't, but I can

Thank You

Thank you to the mean girls
I'm glad I wasn't cool
If that meant scrawling insults
In the toilets back in school

Thank you to the jokers
Who laughed with vicious glee
"He wants to be your boyfriend"
Then said no-one would want me

Thank you to the teacher
Who told me I was lazy
When my anxious thoughts and feelings
Had convinced me I was crazy

Thank you to the friends
Who gave nothing but took all
Turned their backs on me the second
What I offered was too small

Thank you, old acquaintances
Your opinions felt like fact
When you gossiped and you slated me
And laughed behind my back

Thank you to the haters
Who love to wait and see
What I say or what I do next
I know you're watching me

Thank you each and every soul
Who burnt me, broke my heart
You gave me fuel to stoke the fire
That lit my love for art

Thank you for the lessons
You carved the path for me
I'm everything I am
Because you're what I'd hate to be

Your Pain is Your Power

Your pain is just your power
Turned inside out and hidden
Under layers of repression
And the feelings you've forbidden

You've pushed it down and sown it up
Burning, hurting, swallowed whole
And now it turns and fights itself
Picks scraps within your soul

It cuts and picks and punches
Works its way into your mind
It taps and pokes and tugs
The thoughts you tried to leave behind

You try to be immovable
A statue; concrete, still
But you're fighting the impossible
You're the prey it needs to kill

The more you try to fight it
Flee or practise playing dead
The more your pain will seep into
The spaces in your head

Your pain needs an escape route
An open door to free itself
From the prison and the torment
Of your failing mental health

Take everything you're feeling
And instead of trapping it
Encourage it to change and move
And grow a little bit

And feel it billow, bursting
A sea of angry foam
Cast it out to find its freedom
From your claustrophobic home

Feel the tingle in your fingertips
The swell inside your soul
As it travels up your body
And relinquishes control

All these years it's been held captive
Many times it's tried to say
*"I just need you to let me out
and I'll be on my way"*

Now that it's been noticed
You can recognise it when
It comes to pay a visit
Tries to talk to you again

But this time you won't grab it
Punish it with no release
You'll smile and with a softness say
We both have found our peace

My Love

Life is not a sprint, my love
Take all the time you need
To discover who you are
Your wild spirit should be freed

Life is no competition
So you needn't try to be
Anything you don't believe in
You need no apology

Life is not a sentence
It's a long, sensory story
Each page written, a moment
Of disaster and of glory

Life is not a fixture
Nor a single work of art
But a beautiful explosion
Of everything that fills your heart

Life is not a schoolbook
But an everlasting lesson
Learn from all you can, my love
And find your own expression

Life is not a stage
You are not here to play a part
There's never a wrong time
To change your role, make a fresh start

Life is not forever
It's a fleeting mystery
And one day you will realise
You will face parts without me

Life will not be perfect,
It can be cruel and unforgiving
But know this above all else, my love
Your life is made for living

Untitled

Like the winds that whisper gently
Through the dappled evening shade
I will find you in the balmy night
Your spirit torn and frayed

Like the swaying summer meadows
A landlocked ocean floor
I will be the tiny wooden boat
That pulls you to the shore

Like the rain that taps your windows
A rhythmic, soothing drum
I will fall for you from clouds and fill
The spaces where you're numb

Like the blackbird lulling daylight
To the edge of ink black night
I will sing your song beside you
Louder still when out of sight

Like the moon that breaks the darkness
And the stars that blink and die
I will wrap you in my aura
Paint your dreams across the sky

Like the first bud flush of Spring
Where all that dies becomes reborn
I will grow a wild rose and then
Protect you from the thorn

Like the wildest winds of Winter
Coursing, weaving, swirling through
When you're barely even standing
That's when I will carry you

Like the equinox and seasons
And the rising of the Sun
Like the years passed by before us
And the ones that have begun

Like the Moon in all her glory
Pulling tides across the sea
Every moment has a purpose
And every You has Me

Believe Me

Believe me when I say
Your illness has an enemy
You have tools to help you beat it
Your own brand of therapy
You are wise to its behaviour
You have caught it out before
You can use your sword and armour
When it's hammering your door
Don't leave it for tomorrow
Don't delay or hesitate
Admit you're tripping, falling
Before you're down and it's too late
You know this beast, you've beat it
You can do it all once more
Take your army and your A-game
And even up the score

Laura Ding-Edwards

Karma

I don't believe in karma
It's a dangerous perception
That living life above reproach
Grants infinite protection

From the trials and the tragedies
The sour, bitter parts
Of life and love and loss
And shattered dreams and broken hearts

Not everyone will feel you
All that shines can also rust
The wings that sent you soaring
Can leave you bleeding in the dust

The ones that once were cheerleaders
Can turn their batons round
And stab you in the back
Then watch you writhing on the ground

No amount of goodness
Or faith, divinity
Can protect you from the worst of life
The negativity

No kindness or compassion
Delays untimely rest
Worlds can crash in moments
Bad things happen to the best

The simple truth is this
You only ever have control
Of the way you process what you get
And how you make you whole

You don't get any option
In the cards that you are given
Your sole responsibility
Is the direction you are driven

You can choose to let it break you
Hate the world, consume yourself
Or use it for your growth
Build a temple with your wealth

Of knowledge and of peace
Authentic positivity
In the worst moments of life
You'll find the best that you can be

Laura Ding-Edwards

Break the Cycle

Can we break the cycle
Of the poisonous recital
Of believing that it's vital
To pin the blame on *"them"*

By buying the plethoric
Toxic gutter press rhetoric
That it is catastrophic
If we open up our hearts

To the innocent and broken
The unheard and unspoken
This nightmare was foretoken
Caused by those who will not suffer

The tragic misdirection
Of our kindness and affection
Obsessive, fierce protection
Of a perfect Old England

Where only those who fit
The description of *"True Brit"*
Have a lifelong free permit
To enjoy the luxuries

Of freedom, opportunity
Safety, love and unity
A job, a home – community
Somewhere we all belong

No-one owns the Earth
Every single child from birth
Is a soul of equal worth
And deserves a chance to shine

Rethink your information
This rich and diverse nation
Needs a big ego deflation
About who we think we are

Laura Ding-Edwards

Inner Child

Amidst the regularity of adulthood routine
Take a moment
Stop; be still
And sit within the space between

Listen very carefully; a tiny quiet sound
Feint and soft
And waiting 'til
Nobody is around

You can't quite make it out at first, a springing babbling song
It skips and trips
And floats and grows
Leaps happily along

Then stronger and more audible, you start to recognise
Familiar tones
And innocence
Life through a child's eyes

The little voice is you; a tiny friend who long since lost
The playful heart
And longing
For great joy at any cost

Reaching adulthood's a blessing not all folk make it this far
But that free
Curious child
Is exactly who you are

Unencumbered by reality, a world that you create
Each day a gift
No knowledge of
Corruption or such hate

That we see and feel daily, everywhere we turn
But the child
If you listen
Will help you to return

To the beauty of the here and now, existing in the moment
No worries of
What happens next
A beautiful component

Listen out when you feel monotonous and dull
Believe yourself
When little you
Says life is magical

Respect

Homesick for a place
With no hard proof of its existence
An army marching forward
That only meets its own resistance
Bound and gagged and tethered
By one's own unruly mind
A missing piece, a lost part
Something unknown left behind
Grief without bereavement
Shame with no known sin
Apocalyptic unrest
Fire and torment deep within
A primal, wild response
To a modern mind and world
A fear of fear itself
All the lines and boundaries blurred
No rationale or order
A lawless, loveless land
Painful to describe
Impossible to understand
A chemical imbalance
Not a character defect
And those who live this nightmare
Have my ultimate respect

The Unravelling

Bring me your tears
And I will raise you an endless ocean
Wide as it is wild
Deep as it is powerful
Fierce yet undisturbed

Bring me your fragmented spirit
And I will bind you with the trees
Root you to the earth
Your arms outstretched and open
Ready to receive

Bring me your exhausted soul
And I will reawaken your magic
Like the crisp morning
That follows
The longest, darkest night

Bring me your frustrated mind
And I will smother the flames
Dampen your embers
Blow away ash
And soothe your burns

Bring me your whispering heart
And I will show you a lioness
Caged and bound too long
Bursting from your chest
Untamed and unrivalled

Bring me what you have
And I will show you
The unravelling which is necessary
To weave your dreams
Amongst the stars

Unpolished

There's magic in your bones
For I can see it when you smile
And you could see it too
If you would stop and look a while

There's beauty in your flaws
A pure uniqueness no-one equals
Only one of you exists
With no returns, reruns or sequels

There's power in your stories
Every moment you are living
The losses and the lessons
And the grace to keep on giving

There's fire in your heart
A primal longing; not a choice
The fierce soul within you
Speaks for those who have no voice

There's peace amongst your chaos
Quiet calmness in the storm
Dig down a little deeper
Feel your energy transform

Your vivid vulnerability
Bared for the world to see
Perfect human imperfection
You are unpolished, rough edged; free

Prose

Friendship

There is a common theory that your real friends will be there during the hard times.

I've discovered that the truest friends, the kindest hearts and the most loving souls are actually the ones who will comfort you in your bad times but also cheer you on in your good times.

Misery loves company and not everyone who is with you at your lowest is ready to see you grow and blossom.

Real friends will sit with you in the dark and dance with you in the light.

Accountability

It is always ok to be sad, angry, hurt, apathetic, withdrawn, alone and quiet.

It is never, ever ok to be cruel.

Having a mental illness or past trauma or current problems is not your get out clause to treat people badly.

People who have known nothing but pain have offered nothing but kindness.

People who suffer with crippling, debilitating illnesses give everything they have to people who need it.

People who are going through silent heartbreak still open their arms to others.

Your pain is your power. You can either use it to do good or hide behind it. The world does not owe you anything, you can either let your past define you or choose to learn from it, process it and take responsibility for your future.

Waiting

Stop holding out for *"the moment"*. You know what I mean.

"If I could just..."
"I'd be happy if..."
"I only need..."
"I've got to..."

The minute you stop striving for that moment; that perfection; that thing you think will complete your puzzle you start to realise that you can make wholeness from what you already have.

I'm talking about the little things that we make bigger than they should be – the housework, perfect body, the last little bit of fat on your tummy that won't shift.

Please stop putting so much energy into thinking that if these things are done or different that you will feel the completeness you are craving. Hold what you have and feel the fullness of the things that matter.

Friendship
Freedom
Security
Love

Your own beautiful heart.

The moment is right now, if you just turn your eyes away from what you think you need and look at what you already have.

Comfort Zone

You already know which path you need to take. It's the one that feels least comfortable

Pride

There is no pride in love.

Love will bend you and twist you out of shape. It will make you apologise when you really don't want to.

Love will make you feel like you have no control over your emotions.

Love is exciting and terrifying. It will make you hold a mirror up to yourself and question whether you are being the best version of you.

Love will sometimes serve you, sometimes not.

Love will hurt you, even when you think it's good.

Love will make you feel like nothing else matters, because at times it really doesn't. It will fill you up and wring you out and make you feel pathetic and powerful.

Love isn't for the feint hearted. It is tough and troublesome, but it is the only thing worth fighting for; as long as you are both fighting for it.

Love is the only thing we have left when everything else is gone.

Love is the only thing that survives far beyond ourselves.

Laura Ding-Edwards

Gratitude

Stay thankful, even when you have nothing.
Stay humble, even when you have it all.
Stay loyal, even when you have opportunity.
Stay kind, even when you have been hurt.

Reality

Life isn't all sunshine and roses and floaty kindness full of positivity and loveliness. There are very few people in this world who are so enlightened that they can allow every aspect of life to wash over them with no reaction. Not everything deserves a reaction; but some things do and sometimes that reaction is "f*ck it". It's cathartic to keep it real.

Endings

Sometimes we fall apart so we can put ourselves back together better. Endings are not always a bad thing; we can use them to reflect and rejuvenate and restart. There is absolutely no shame in falling apart, just don't stay there.

It's an opportunity to do things differently.

Individuality

Learn to love your realness.

Your "imperfect" teeth, your hair that doesn't do what you want it to, your stretch marks or scars, your nose that isn't quite right. These things make you unique; they make you perfectly you.

You are the only you in the whole universe.

How amazing is that?

Enabling

Enablement feels and looks and sounds a lot like Love.

And it IS Love, but in order to really save someone from themselves you need to allow them the freedom to move as far away from who they are as possible.

Maybe they will come back, or maybe all you have done is free them and yourself from your hopes of who they could be.

Either way, you cannot fix someone who has no reason or motivation to heal. If being broken has always worked, then why would they change that?

There are times when we think we are rescuing someone, when all we are actually doing is allowing them to drown us to stay afloat.

Empathy

Sympathy says *"I feel sorry for you"*

But empathy says *"I am you."*

Heal

When we make the same mistakes over and over again, the most important question we can ask ourselves is "what wound do I need to heal to set myself free?"

Aware

The first part of growth is accountability. Holding your hands
up to your flaws and faults and striving to change. We are all
programmed to find fault in others to make ourselves feel better
and it's in our nature to compare and compete; making a conscious
decision to pull ourselves up when we do this unnecessarily is
a really important part of moving away from needing to pitch
ourselves against others.

Light

If someone is throwing shade at you, don't you dare dim your light –
turn and shine in the other direction.

Peace

True friendship is worth fighting for, but the fact is you should never have to .

Don't be afraid to take steps to remove yourself from people who don't benefit your mental health, even if you have history. Your peace is your priority.

Authenticity

Is there a more boring thing to be than normal?
Be incredible, be ridiculous, be unique.

Be so unashamed of your authenticity that you allow everyone
around you to embrace their perceived abnormalities and wear
them like a crown

Body

Nobody will stand up at your funeral to talk about your clothes size.

Please stop living like it's that important

Allowance

Stop trying to figure it all out.

Stop trying to second guess.

Stop trying to plan for every single possible outcome.

Stop thinking you have control over anything but your own behaviour.

Stop thinking your thoughts are your reality.

Stop ruining now with future worries and past memories.

Stop and just be with whatever you are feeling right now.

Even if it feels overwhelming, let it come, and let it go.

Eventually it will free you.

Deflection

Remember this when thinking about those who hurt you;

It must be a lonely, dark and bleak world to live in when you are consumed by jealousy and suspicion.

It must be a miserable and torturous existence, if you feel that the only way you can survive is by tearing down other people.

It must be tiring having to find someone to hate and direct your anger towards.

Imagine using deflection over self analysis, over and over again.

When faced with these people, don't try to reason. Don't get drawn in to the toxicity of it all. Not everything needs a resolution for you to move on from it.

Sometimes it's so much better to accept that they are not emotionally mature enough to face their wounds – instead they cut you.

Remove yourself and heal, not everyone is comfortable working through pain in order to find a different way of coping.

Leave them to fight it out between themselves.
Take a breath, remember who you are and let it be.

Life

The biggest mistake we all make is thinking of "Life" as an end result.

"Life".

As if it's this magical thing that happens when we have everything in order.

We are always working towards an end goal, as if miraculously once we get there we get "Life" and everything stops and stays exactly as it is in that perfect moment when we've got everything "done" or "finished".

We go to school and dream about this wonderful thing called "Life" that happens when we grow up. But so often we spend it looking for the next thing to do before we can enjoy it.

Life is not the prize at the end of a test. It's not a destination at the end of a long journey. It's not a reward for working harder than others in a job you hate.

Life is right now.

It's happened, is happening, and is going to happen, every second you are still breathing.

If you change your perception, your language, your feelings on it, you will realise that everything that has been, everything that will be and everything you are experiencing right this second IS Life.

It is so fleeting and fragile, fluid and powerful - so often we take it for granted and miss it completely. All you have is right now - Life is now.

Laura Ding-Edwards

Self Esteem

The only people who gain from your low self-esteem are the people who want to keep you there. Lift your head, your heart and your standards and watch how the deadwood drifts away on its own.

Hype

Help each other up – hype each other up.

Self-Reflection

Don't confuse self-reflection with self-criticism.

There is such a big difference between looking at a situation and exploring what you can learn from it and beating yourself up.

Growth is all about reflection. It sounds like kind advice to yourself and gentle encouragement.

What it doesn't sound like is negative feedback;

"Everything I do is wrong"
"Why do I always mess everything up"
"I must be a bad person"

Change the way you do this – stop using language that makes you feel like a victim of your own behaviour.

"What can I learn from this"
"How can I adapt my approach"
"What can I do differently in future"

And most importantly, sometimes it is entirely valid to accept that actually, you did everything right and your only mistake was not trusting your intuition.

Toxicity

You can send out as much good as you want to toxic people, yet they will still find a way to turn it into poison.

Don't waste your time or energy unnecessarily unpacking your intentions, when you know in your heart you were doing right. If someone else has an agenda, they will twist whatever you do to fit, and there is absolutely nothing you can do to change that.

If whatever you give out is met with hatred, then your actions will never be received with love.

If your goodness is rearranged by someone to suit their needs, that's not your problem.

As much as you want to change this, you can't. Stop giving these people ammunition.

If there is one thing you need to know and truly believe it is this;

Not
Everyone
Likes
Peace

When nothing you do is good enough, the best thing to do is nothing at all.

Laura Ding-Edwards

Burning

You know what's really badass? Being dragged through hell, coming out the other end & not feeling the need to go around burning everyone else. Remaining soft in a hard world takes real strength.

Your Heart

Don't keep breaking your own heart over people who wouldn't break silence for you.

Permission

Do not fear your talents just because other people do.

You have permission to bloom.

Reassurance

The next time you feel your anxiety rising, know this;

It cannot hurt you.

I know it feels like your heart is going to explode, your sense of reality is off kilter; your adrenaline is coursing and making you feel like you're going to lose it; you feel sick, dizzy and like you're going to pass out and die.

You're really, *really* not.

The funny thing about anxiety is that its whole purpose is to protect you.

Imagine how unhelpful our defence mechanism would be if it made us drop down dead. Think about how ridiculous that is for a second. You see a tiger, your body goes into fight or flight mode, and you die. How pointless would that be?

Next time you feel it, try really hard not to fear it. Be kind to it, thank it for protecting you but reassure it that it's not needed right now, and you can handle things just fine on your own.

Sit with it and allow it to peak, because I'll tell you what happens on the other side of a panic attack – absolutely nothing. It literally just goes away again. And yes, it might come back. But again, all that will happen is that it will peak and then it will pass.

I promise you, the first time you sit alongside it and allow it to do its worst, you will see that there is nothing to fear from it at all.

Rawness

If you are tiptoeing around, then you are walking amongst the wrong people.

Seek out those who appreciate raw honesty; who know that your opinion is valid, important and comes from a good place.

Growth

There is nothing more magical than watching people you love bravely stepping out of their comfort zone, embracing their power and fulfilling their potential. It's so infectious – the more you see people do it, the more people you want to see do it.

It works on a different level too, in that it gives a wider circle the confidence to reach into their deepest self and ask the questions they never dared to before.

Encouraging growth, change and authenticity is such a beautiful and fulfilling experience for everyone that you just can't help but want to spread it as far as possible.

Embrace

There are days when you will wake up and your anxiety or depression has kindly decided to give you a day off.

These are the days to practise the things you feel you can't do when you're poorly – push your boundaries, move out of your comfort zone. Prove to your body and your brain that life isn't as scary or pointless as it seems on the days you are unwell.

Snatch a victory – it will keep you going on the bad days.

Empowerment

Empower yourself to accept what is;

Apologies you never got.
Goodbyes you never said.
I Love Yous that weren't reciprocated

You won't always get the luxury of closure, practice how to be ok with that.

Loyalty

Take good care of the people who talk about you as if you were always beside them.

True loyalty is so grounding, there is such beauty in trusting someone enough to know that if you weren't around they would still sing your song.

Power

Listen carefully to what your haters are saying about you – there is your power.

Strength

Take strength from the Moon, who even in darkness knows she is still whole.

Imagine

For maybe it is not anxiety that fills your bones after all.

Maybe it is a deep and ancient magic that weaves throughout you, shackled for too long by the confines of this modern world, occupying the space within you that some only dare to dream exists.

Silence

The path to success brings with it raw exposure.

Those who are truly happy for you will shine your light publicly privately, consistently.

Those who aren't will speak volumes in their silence. Pay close attention; these are the people who will only speak up once you reach your destination.

The people who believe in you from the first step, not the last, are the ones who matter most.

Conflict

There is a conflict in all of us when it comes to right and wrong and we owe it to ourselves to appreciate that not everyone experiences this in the same way.

Most of us understand right and wrong to a point, but this moral and social responsibility can sometimes be outweighed by what feels good for us rather than the greater good.

When people compromise on their morality to fulfil their own needs this can be down to so many different factors and experiences – more often than not it's a combination of lots of different things.

We must all practice suspending our judgment and disregarding what we think as normal. We have all lived different experiences, through different eyes and different perspectives and we all possess varying levels of emotional connection to ourselves.

If someone is choosing their own needs above the "right" thing to do then it is often because they don't possess the presence of mind to understand the wider implications. Or maybe they do, but they feel this isn't as relevant to them as it is to other people.

Think about this next time you are about to judge someone on their behaviour, lifestyle choices or way of dealing with their problems; not everyone has the luxury of awareness beyond the here and now. Opening lines of communication, engaging, asking questions and really listening to the answers is the only way we can all work towards understanding other people's view of the world.

We are only ever able to work with the tools we have in the present moment, be patient.

Space

That pit of the stomach feeling, deep chest burning we feel when we are going through difficult times; that's our soul making space for better things.

Trust

In twelve months time you will look back and be so glad that you stuck around for the good stuff.

Where you are now is not where you will always be. Trust in the process.

My Anxiety

When I say "my anxiety is bad today" what I don't mean is "I'm worrying more than normal".
What I mean is that I am experiencing a whole array of uncomfortable physical symptoms that have no known trigger.

My primal brain is reading movement, memories, normal everyday things, stuff on TV, sounds, smells and sights as an actual threat to my survival and is reacting accordingly, within a split second, to keep me alive. Over and over and over again.

Of course my rational "daily brain" knows what is going on, but it actually isn't working properly because my primal "anxious brain" has taken over - my "anxious brain" and my "daily brain" are two completely separate parts.

Brains don't actually wait to find out if the threat is real or not, it just reacts. I know this can't kill me, I know it can't hurt me, I know it's absolutely there to protect me, but it is almost impossible to function normally when your whole existence is currently in survival mode.

Here's what you really need to hear and believe - ANXIETY IS NOT A CHOICE. It's not just being nervous, it's not just worrying about something, it is a physiological disorder that causes very real, very physical sensations. What you are experiencing during high anxiety is your brain's reaction to a perceived threat to your survival.

As an example, sometimes when my anxiety is really bad I can't even move as it will trigger my adrenaline. I have to find a comfortable position and then stay there until I can bring everything down a level. I have to unplug the house phone and turn off my mobile so that they don't go off, as this can trigger me. Eating or drinking can trigger me. Going to the toilet can trigger me. This comes and goes across the hour, day, or week, but when it peaks it really is this sensitive.

It takes an incredibly strong person to experience these sensations coming and going without reacting to them. To be able to sit with anxiety and allow it to peak and trough as it needs to while you force your rational brain back on and your anxious primal brain back off takes practice and an immense amount of mental strength and clarity. This system of "fight or flight" is buried deep within our brains and has been vital to the survival of humans for thousands of years. Anyone who is able to experience and ignore the sensations and physical reactions that are triggered by the brain's survival mechanism deserves a massive amount of respect.

The next time someone calls in sick to work, or cancels plans, or leaves a situation because their anxiety is bad; please don't think they are sat at home being "a bit worried about stuff". I can personally vouch for the fact that they will be feeling incredibly physically poorly, (nausea/vomiting, dizziness, blurred vision, muscle twitches, heart palpitations, sense of being in a dream) and it really isn't to do with worry. It is to do with the primal part of the brain being on overdrive.

You owe it to yourself to really understand the meaning of clinical anxiety, because I guarantee you will think very differently of the people who suffer with it.

Resources and Support

If you are struggling with your mental health or emotional wellbeing, please reach out to someone.

The following organisations and resources all have mental health at the heart of their mission:-

The Frank Bruno Foundation

Aims to provide support, encouragement and the motivation to succeed for those experiencing or recovering from mental ill-health

www.thefrankbrunofoundation.co.uk

Mind

Empowers people to understand their condition and the choices available to them.

www.mind.org.uk

The Happiness Project

The Happiness Project is a peer to peer support group, They create and host a number of social events that aim to create a strong social support network to eradicate the isolation and loneliness often felt when battling mental health.

www.facebook.com/THPMCR

Samaritans

Free and confidential helpline and webchat open 24 hours a day, 365 days a year. Working together to make sure fewer people die by suicide.

www.samaritans.org

CALM (Campaign Against Living Miserably)

Free and confidential helpline and webchat. Leading a movement against suicide.

www.thecalmzone.net

SASP (Support After Suicide Project)

Supporting those bereaved by suicide.

www.suportaftersuicide.org.uk

Time to Change

Changing how we think and act about mental health problems.

www.time-to-change.org

Young Minds

Fighting for young people's mental health

www.youngminds.org.uk

About the author

Laura Ding-Edwards is an artist and writer from Herefordshire, UK.

She started her business, Rainbird Roots, in 2016 and quickly went from painting as a hobby to full-time artist, commissioning pet portraits, unique wildlife artwork & typography pieces. The Rainbird Roots brand name comes from her mother's beautiful maiden name of "Rainbird". You can see Laura's artwork by visiting www.rainbirdroots.com.

Her first poem, The Mountain, was written in a car back in January 2019 and details her experiences of living with anxiety. It rapidly gained momentum on social media, having had millions of views and shares across the world. From this, more poems were written and eventually The Mountain book was born.

Laura lives with her husband, Ronnie, and continues to write and paint alongside spending time with her two horses, Bess and Chester, whom she credits with being the source of her most peaceful moments in life.

Follow Laura on social media;

Facebook: Rainbird Roots - Laura Ding-Edwards

Instagram & Twitter: @rainbirdroots

Get in touch: info@rainbirdroots.com